the soul breathes solitude

...and other poems

by alex b. diamond

for Uncle Lou

...you always made sure to be there for me

Contents

a poem of love for all humanity

love is...
two people, walking together…
maybe, oh, let's say...just holding hands
and if they are slowly beginning to
tumble down, and free fall into love..?
that's a wonderful thing!
and that means everything is gonna feel wonderful soon!
everything in all of our hearts is
gonna work out real soon, my friends!
I know it, and you know it!
I know it for sure, and as for you?
you!
you, the beautiful, vulnerable, and imperfect person…
may have doubts, and that's okay!
that's okay, humanity!
truly!
really!
you can
feel any doubt, any emotion there is, you people!
why did you ever suppose feeling an emotion
was wrong to begin with, you people?
can you recall the first time you supposed feeling an
emotion, or feeling, was wrong to do, you guys?
well, can you, or not?
if not, it's okay, don't worry about it
things will turn out okay!
I promise!
there is plenty of time for love!
there is plenty of time for love of all humanity!

I am totally sure of it, my friends!
yes!
yes indeed!
so...
what are you gonna do about it
people?
what are you gonna do
about love
right
now?
do
something!
love
someone!
now!
ah ha ha ha ha ha ha ha!
I love you, baby!
yes…
I really do...
mwah!

I write the painting that hangs

you are not my enemy, darling
I have no time for that
for fights
my life is not a trampoline, I don't bounce
for kicks
I try, I try, to glide
like a gull on the lip of a subtle sea breeze
cool in the caribbean waters
because, I love it
and
I love you
girl of the cryptic smile
biting your lip so slightly
with furrowed brow
and
tapping fingers on
the formica
sip your coffee slowly, dear
and
hit your morning smoke
I don't mind, in fact
I love that too
cause the wisps always curl up in ribbons
surrounding your face in a cloud
of
timeless
beauty…

cigarette after cigarette

sweaty lonely nights
without you
drizzle rain
inside my room
I pace the electric floor, breathing
sighing
with the weight of loss
I wish I had my love back
seeking more from you
return, please, now
with bitter memories jaded
in the sharpest cut, no time for regret
allow our nest to grow in heat
and sweltering conditions
what did I say?
it must have been really bad
to cause this avalanche of grief
misled in a moment of fallen whimsy
I couple myself with terror, tonight
and dream of an escape so daring
scaling the walls of my heartache
to reach for you...

close the door with tenderness, next time

I dreamt of you
again
this time in a white, sheer nightgown
on a gentle, grassy hill
silhouetted against the moonlight
like a night angel
calling to me softly
stay with me
stay with me
stay with me...

are the streets quiet tonight?

these chords are the harmony of our city
these strings are the sound of our songs
sing them as you like
cause
they are ultimately all we got these days
and for me it's not too bad
and for me, I still have hope, a lot of hope for us
if you can see fit to trust me
and the way we sang our words
that week, that month, that day
then I can say
yes
yes
we're gonna have plenty of victories
together
over these adversities
at least I will
at least he will
at least they will and they will
and those folks over there will
so hey
relax
the city loves you well enough
and
you know what else?
the
city
is quiet tonight...

the soul breathes solitude

when I am alone
I smoke
when I am alone
I pace
when I am alone
I think
when I am alone
I sip
when I am alone
I sing
when I am alone
time crawls by
when I am alone
the phone rings robots
when I am alone
the light shines in the windows blinding me
and
when I am alone
the earth breathes without me
and
life goes on...

an ode to the littlest music box

a tinkling sound, louder still
encompassing the world
the quick curiosity of a little boy
the treasure of a little girl
the fortunes of a thousand men
and deaths of thousands more
went into making this music box
which sits inside a store
and on a weary, dreary, rainy, snowy, winter's day
someone picks up this little toy
and opens it to hear it play
the angels fall out of the sky
and sprinkle on the plains
the asteroids and the meteors, too
and all the dead remains
the kaleidoscopic drumbeat of a literal translation
and carnival tickets ripped in half
on the campgrounds of a nation
can all be taken as a whole
forced into a little gold box
and play a simple children's song...

why does the man in the car go by so often back and forth?

I was sitting around
just doing nothing
hanging out by myself
not particularly thinking about anything major
and, what happened was, I heard a voice
not a loud voice, or a harsh voice
or an angry voice
but someone
saying things to me calmly and quietly
important things
at first I was a little startled
spooked even, I'll admit
I quickly decided, cause
I was still in my being a man phase
I'm gonna talk back and reply back
and see what this voice has to say
answer it and converse
in my own way, being myself
so I says, I says, yeah, what's up
what do you want?
and the voice gets real little and real real quiet
and says
do what you want to do and you will be fine for a long long time
you will win
go for it…

an ode to little girls

honey, listen to me well
your mother's world is not your hell
I know it's swell to scream and yell
but button pushing I can tell
now, if you think your luck is bad
and you don't like your mom or dad
you're right, they're really not that great
but trust me kid, it's not too late
achieve a state of bliss and comfort
be a kid and rise above it
or, if you can be like the boys, you'll love it
run and play and laugh and sing
skip and dance and do your thing
there is no need to start no trouble
chew your gum and blow your bubble
look inside the inner sanctum
there you'll see the real salvation
colossal threats are always looming
life contains much more than grooming
cars can do something other than zooming
the premise, which is to take you places
get you stuff and show you faces
reach the summit, you won't plummet
stop, continue, then you'll see
everybody loves you
you really are beautiful
and
free…

I miss Jeff Griffith!

guys!
what the fuck is up with Jeff?
I haven't seen him in a dog's age!
where the hell is hiding out at?!
I wanna see that dude, guys!
what the fuck!
I love Jeff!
I know, he is cool
right?
totally
Jeff rocks, man!
he can wail on an electric, man!
he's really good on an electric guitar, man, for real
I heard him play many times
he absolutely fucking shreds!
he coulda been a rock star, but
he chose medicine instead
I know
that's pretty fuckin' noble of him, if ya ask me
yeah, that's true, I agree
he coulda been huge
straight up, but
yeah
I think, like, everyone who can be a doctor, like
they can do it, and shit?
they do it
they become doctors
it's like a code
it's important, you know, it's a super heavy, super

important job
that's true
Jeff's kind of a genius, isn't he?
what do you guys think? Jen?
yeah
I'd say so
I mean, he rips on guitar, man
he can play fast, and he can, like, tweak out the strings and
play all soulful, and shit
he does it all
whatever happened to his band?
The Dust Bunnies, right?
like, rockin' funk with his awesome soloing
all over the place, and shit?
yeah, they were dope, man!
I think they're just on hiatus
Jeff's working long hours as a doctor, it's a
big committment
he's a saint for that, though, I mean, right?
yeah, man, for real
that's awesome of him
I woulda chosen the rock star life
if it had been me, fuck that!
I know, right? me too!
guys, I miss him!
he's so busy, I can't reach him!
he's not returning my calls!
I know, I tried him, too, a while back
I don't blame him
he's busy
I miss him, though!
I love Jeff a lot, he's an awesome guy, guys!
come on!

what the fuck, guys?!
it's making me sad!
I think I'm gonna cry!
Jeff is a beautiful cat, you guys!
I wanna see him!
like, what's up with that?
I know
yeah, I know, I know, for real, miss that guy, man
it'll be alright, Tommy!
yeah, Tom! don't worry about it!
okay
it's cool
it kinda sucks, though, cause he's funny as shit, too
right? hell yeah!
remember how he used to just have us fuckin' dying with his
Bill Clinton impression?
I feel your brain!
ahhh!
that was hilarious!
fuckin' Jeff, man!
fuckin' a, man, he rocks!
fuck it, man, I'm just gonna call him and
leave a message
let him know we miss him
he'll see it
that's true
Jeff Griffith is a dope friend, one way or the other, though
is he gonna come around soon, though?
what do you think, Pam?
hmm...I mean, maybe?
I don't know, it would be nice to see him, though...
tell you what, I'm gonna write him a
snail-mail letter, tellin' him we're thinking of him

and miss him, and
you guys all sign it, too
and
we'll see what happens
like, if he comes around
what do you guys think? cool?
Faith? sound good?
you've been quiet, what do you think?
I love Jeff, I'd fuckin' love to see him, count me in, I'm down for
whatever, Jeff rocks!
he's very handsome, too, I always thought
did you ever hook up with him, Faith?
yeah, a couple times
he's very sexy
I know, totally
right?
damn
cool
good old Jeff Griffith!
freakin' cool guy!
yeah...
love that guy!

the sickness is better than The Cure

no
not exactly
what's the disease ravaging your system?
alienation?
boredom and depression?
feeling unaccepted, unapproved, and rejected?
cursed to be weird, different, strange?
awkward, and over-emotional?
misunderstood, lost, and adrift
in a black sea of nothingness?
basically, you're longing
to
be
understood, and accepted
for
who
you
are?
an artistic, sensitive soul
living in suburbia, or
a small town in
the middle of nowhere?
surrounded by white quasi-thugs, bullies, jocks, and
trendies, prom queens, and sheeple?
you
want
to
be
loved

but
your
parents and family
are
icebergs?
well...
it's not acceptance you really desire, I say
it's community
and a chance
at
self-expression, that
is actually communication
cause
people listen, or see it...
it gets across...
you just
need
to
move!

atrophy atrocity

...you need a massage, baby!
can't you see your musculature is
simply
languid?
in a word-
atrophied!
you need someone to kneed, and rub, and
squeeze you
all
over! all over!
break up those dense and underutilized
flesh deposits!
you must ache all over!
you must have a continual migraine!
you must be nauseous, and
practically ulcerative in
your gut!
your little tummy!
stretch! massage yourself!
I mean, this is
quite
obvious, to
me!

all the way to the crescendo, then down down down

my oh my, I get high
yes, it's a stoner's life for me, you see
yes, yes, yes, love it, love it
squeeze all the resin out of the fig fruit
try not to care
but I do
nope, nope, I never feel blue inside
or either giddy at the prospect
when the meaning slips through our grubby little fingers
we cry out
oh! that wasn't what I meant to do!
mistakes always happen
cause man is so weak
so disillusioned sometimes
be my girlfriend, yeah?
like you I like you and only you you alone
perhaps it's a mutual feeling
then we can kiss each other
with the very last bit of love
in the world
before the crows peck out our red red eyes
and the grave digger lights a smoke
and leans on his shovel
he is the last and final
arbiter
of hearts cascading through time
till the sun burns out
and gravity collapses in on itself
folding up our shadows
in the night...

not nowhere

many poems are short or long
sometimes you just write a song
when the wind mess up your hair
then you know you belong there
all these artists with their tales
some are giants, some just snails
but when the man beats down your door
you'll know it's all been said before
different people have their ways
of getting through the winter days
but people like me who sing loud
will always show how to be proud
come along on a different path
we may cry, and we may laugh
but life is not so hard to bear
as long as you live in a place somewhere...
not nowhere
not nowhere...

this girl made me lose my shit

I was dating this fine chick named Jenny Harper
for about three months
plump short little curly blonde thing
with a pretty smile
and enthusiastic eyes
educated
artistic and a world traveler
23 years old
beautiful
I had just said I love you to her for the first time the previous
night
and she had returned it, and I was over the moon
ecstatic
then, out of nowhere, she was like,
we need to talk
and I felt my stomach drop
and I thought to myself
oh damn
what's this gonna be all about?
fuck me
I'm scared
I hope she doesn't wanna split up
I don't want this chick to dump me now
I just fell in love with her last week
and, to reiterate, told her as much just yesterday
okay, calm down, take a few breaths,
no need to be phony and hide them,
take a breath and say something casual,
like…well, choose your own vernacular, but

say
what is it dear?
in those exact words
I thought all that in a split second and prepared to respond
I spoke:
oh? what's up, babe?
and then, without a nano-second's
hesitation, she dropped the bomb:
I'm dumping you
I wanna break up
I'm sorry
it's over
we're through
well, needless to say and as you can imagine, I completely lost
my shit
matter of fact, I went off the deep end
might as well say, I blew my top, or
to put it another way
I flipped my wig
I started screaming my head off like a complete psycho
and babbling incoherently like a raving lunatic
b-b-b-but....what?!
I mean, I, what!?
I felt totally fucked
and my heart was ripped into ten million pieces which were spit
on and stomped on in a millisecond
damn was I heated!
I picked up the nearest lamp and smashed it against the wall
then I let out a long howl like a rabid coyote in the moonlight
at this she replied
sorry man
shit happens
I was livid

I screamed at the top of my lungs
whyyy!!!
whyyy Lord!!!
I was completely blowing a gasket
basically, I lost my ever-lovin' mind over this shit
I was psychotic
so, I dropped to my knees with
the last shred of sanity
in my very being
and begged her
please don't go please!
I love you so much!
I'll die without you!
I'll instantaneously have a massive coronary cardiac event, a
heart attack
if you move one millimeter!
stay!
I was having serious chest pains at this point
and sweating like a pig
plus, I was shaking and twitching all over
and my vision was going in and out, I was seeing spots
also, I was very lightheaded and thought I was going to pass out
I managed to croak out
one last dying desperate word, gasping
before the blackness closed in
please
and she said
well…
okay
if It means that much to you
I'll stay, baby
I like you you know
I just wanted to move on

and find someone even better
I'd had enough
but I'll waste some time for you
together longer
and I managed to spit out
thank you lover
the love of my life
I'll kill myself anyway if that's what you want
help me
learn to
love
and
I will let you go then with no qualms
baby
sweet ambrosia
and
nectar of my world
my fantasy girl
and dream girl
and partner
and
friend
I love you so much
woman
tell me you love me too..?
I do
I really really do
my wonderful godlike stud
my heart
and
my soulmate
forevermore…

when the moon is all you got

if nothing ever comes along
to
mend my broken heart
so be it
I'll soldier on
fruitlessly, perhaps, but
yeah
I'll make it
I'll be alright
just gotta wait, is all
training my rifle at the sunrise
ready to obliterate the source of my dismay
a ghost of myself
beating the drum for victory
against all odds
you know how the story goes, don't you?
boy meets girl, boy gets girl, boy loses girl, boy loses hope
boy remains
girl escapes
then
it rains
then
the downpour soaks the whole city
and
the flowers of love spring forth
in a dazzling array of hues and shades
hearts harbor hope as well
and the clouds part in grey
furious at themselves

for living
and for dying
forlorn
and
for love…

an ode to Depeche Mode

...if you are even dreaming of me giving up on my band
let me tell you loud and proud I will always be a fan
cause the songwriting is impeccable
and the whole sound is incredible
and if you wind up missing on a milk carton
then you know you will be found by Martin
and also if you are a slave, then Dave will be like yo!
just listen to my steady tenor voice and you will really know
that I am great singer, and the fact that I can dance is true
and don't worry, it's only the first listen that we make you blue
after that you will return to dig our amazing soundscapes
and our cover art is so dope it even looks good on tapes
now, it may be true that after '86 they were kinda spotty
but that was just a short hiatus for Fletch to learn karate
so they could save money on bouncers, and not need the Hell's
Angels
for the Rose Bowl show which was filmed from many angles
and the crowd was super unified for the crescendo of Everything
Counts
and, well, that took care of capitalism, so now weed sells by the
ounce
no more drinking pints and eating nasty fish and chips
and now there's some decent girls in England, big tits, nice hips
for the guys to have big families, and even pay Alan Wilder
for his real musical chops, plus the weather is much milder
so from the days of being pop tarts, not real, but pretend
the synthesizer boy band has always been my one true friend!!!

another night in the wilds

there is no tomorrow, is how I live
nothing else will suffice
how can I be so sure?
well, it's largely instinct
these are my tools
some are bronze some are stone
I am early man
hominid
and I know what the whole future of my life looks like
and it's a waste
a boring drudge and burden
I need paint
I need food and bear pelts
I need a cave to warm up in and stay the night
with my clan
and with my fire
cooking meat
why is this good?
I can't quite say
but I watch the stars
and sing a winsome
blues...

an ode to the great New Order

well, damn, what can you really say?
I immediately fell in love with them the first time I pushed play
on my little boom box in '85, it was Power, Corruption, and Lies
and I asked my New Wave mentor, Jess, who the hell are these
guys?
this is freaking amazing, I right away was gushing
yes, the music was so dope, they could've been singing in
Russian
for all I cared, and yes, I played that tape to pieces
I'd probably even worship Bernard Sumner, before I'd pray to
Jesus
if you think I am exaggerating, give that disc a spin
it hits you hard right from the first riff, like a right hook to the
chin
and never lets up for a second, in the nine songs after that
now 35 years later, I still rock it in my flat
it's like a drug, this band New Order, of the New Wave sound
Technique is fucking incredible, too, with Fine Time, and Round
And Round
Low-Life is killer, and Substance '87- a masterpiece
they utterly kick the shit outta more famous bands like The Police
you see, they got these dope ass songs, that I call 'monster jams'
with complex percussion crescendos, that are made with eight
strong hands
three guys and one girl, Bernard, Peter, Stephen, and Gillian
and if I should ever meet them, all I could say is thanks a million!
I shouldn't neglect to say that their style is truly art
cause the song titles are all just poetry, straight from England's
heart

Manchester is the city, that they alone put on the map
and people that say they prefer Joy Division, I would like to slap
for jumping on the Goth bandwagon, of that subpar incarnation
shame? state? no, they are the geniuses of the nation!
so play Blue Monday one more time, or the remix of Bizarre
Love Triangle
and savor that sweet, sweet music that is timeless, almost every
single
and four amazing albums that you can never, ever tire of
and that is why New Order is a great, great band which I love!!

there are many times I fucked up, this is so true

yes, I have made many mistakes
I mean, yes, I really fucked up a lot of shit
so, yeah, I have many regrets
so, don't feel too bad, all you beautiful, imperfect beings out there
of the gentle human race
it's hard
life
you know, you fuck up sometimes
you hurt others, you hurt yourself
sometimes you scream at folks
sometimes you might even hit someone, or worse
I have, you may have too, and I wanna tell you
it's okay
it's not the end of the world
they'll forgive you, and
you'll bounce back
tomorrow is always a new day
tonight will only last so long, and
you will sleep
you'll sleep again, you will
you know it
and
when you do
you will recharge, and renew, and regain the chance
to do better
or
to be imperfect again, as is your fate
and all of ours
everybody

there is no way to get through life otherwise
learning
and
discovering ourselves as we unfold is a bumpy road
a treacherous path
fraught with troubles and turbulence, hazards and happenstance
and one which we must traverse without foreshadowing or
practice, or even fair warning
no map
no guidebook
you gotta dive in, and just start paddling for all you got
in this life
eventually
you'll get better
smoother
you'll find a way
these things take time
so, fear not
you won't fuck up everything forever
in due time
you will adopt your stroke
and
your rhythm
and
even your style
yes you, you
will one day get nice with this
living
it's gonna be alright
and
when that day comes
everybody will applaud you
as
you
soar...

now I got a handle on it

no morals are needed
and no time is ever spent
bleeding from the heart valve
always gets you rent
courage is essential
when going for the gold
nobody knows different
it's all a lie, we've been told
can you maintain your focus?
in a world of dismal light
when all is lost beforehand
and nothing you do is right
please release your fury
on this a winter day
and just go off the deep end
and just scream out your say
why am I so despondent?
and why am I so blue?
when all you could've responded
was yes, I need you too...

glory be this party just got rocking

no more waiting for the ball to drop
this demands action now
and nobody on the planet earth
can foresee the way things will turn out
but I know
oh yes I know
what in the name of all that is good and holy does God want from
me?!
worship?
obedience?
love?
adulation?
piousness?
or maybe, maybe, maybe
all these people are just waiting
for a man like me to come along
and say
hey
I love you
if there is a God, He loves you
and if the sun were to crash and burn into the steel forests of
babylon
we would all live to rise another day
and another
that much I can promise you
safe…

the ballad of a donut-girl and her unrequited love, part 2

donut-girl: a whiner, one who complains a lot
slice: a very handsome, built, and desirable man

…there once lived a donut-girl, who had a real big crush
upon a slice named Thomas P., who always had to rush
to work and back, then to the gym, so he could lift his weights
and when he took her out to eat, he rushed through all their dates
she soon felt she was in love with him, and she dumped her other
men
she had a lot of other lovers, almost nine or ten
but none of them compared to him, the suitor Thomas P.
and plus he drove a real nice car, and got a big salary
though not quite rich, he was well-off, and showered her with
gifts
plus he played a mean guitar, and knew a lot of riffs
this donut-girl didn't even whine, when he went out of town
because he treated her like a queen, and she loved the sparkling
crown
the two of them together felt like it was really meant to be
they even dared to think of themselves as each other's destiny
cause all their friends got along real well, and they had lots of fun
they even moved into a good neighborhood, safe with a dog and a
gun
she loved her life, this donut-girl, and got a big promotion
from being a local correspondent, to an anchor across the ocean
her job took her to many countries, and she found none better
than France which had some great fromage, but she still loved
her Wisconsin cheddar

and Thomas P., with all his faults, still ran banks with lots of
vaults
and had the keys to all of them, and nobody called more shots
so as a couple they were really sure they were in love
and would always have each other's backs, even when push
came to shove
so, if you are a donut-girl, take this hint from Al Diamond -
just you keep on being you, and one day you will stop whinin'!!!

an ode to white womanhood

ah! the western standard of beauty
oh! the cute blonde with no booty
ah! you live in la la land
hey! I want you to front my band
well, we had ourselves a little fling
you saw me smoke, I heard you sing
flower of white womanhood
Georgia peach, smell so good
crisp and clean and no caffeine
trophy wife for the American Dream
oh so sad, and always giving
I don't understand your reason for living
look in the mirror and be in awe
your pretty face is all we saw...

ladies and gentlemen, The Beatles!

oh yeah I
tell you something
I think you'll understand
when I
say that something
I wanna hold your hand
I wanna hold your hand
I wanna hold your hand...
thank you
well
that was crazy
yeah, I know, mate
I mean
this
this
reaction we're getting
it's fuckin' bonkers, you know
I mean
this is mayhem
Paul
are we really that fuckin' good, mate?
level with me
cause
I'll admit it
I'm a little scared, man
I don't want some young girl, you know
killing herself over us, or something
well, I hear ya, Ringo
I mean, this splash we're making

I think I can say
it's blowing all our minds
right guys?
yeah
oh yeah, definitely
this is wild
it's completely unprecedented
far as I can see, mates
never been nothing like it
like
ever
I gotta say it
we're bigger than Jesus
they're screaming like we're gods, mates
this
is
crazy
man, guys, I just wanted to have a
solid band, guys
play good rock 'n roll
see how long I could last it
before having to
get
a
real
job
I mean
we're all gonna be
millionaires
when our next checks come
I can for sure say that
we'll never have to work again
that's obvious, isn't it?

we can be glad about that
what's it really all about, John?
you're the 'smart one' ha ha
lad from Liverpool
what's it all about, in essence?
I'm ready
tell us, mate
yeah, go on, let's hear it, John
well...
it's about
music
rock 'n roll
music
you see there's gonna be a lot of great bands
and
great singers
to follow us
in
rock 'n roll music
and almost definitely in some
derivative
other
styles, too
music is fundamental
it's hugely moving
hugely joy-causing
and
we
represent the promise
of
much, much
great music
and

great times with dancing and singing and loving
music, mates
that's all I can say
I don't know
hm
well, hey
I don't care about the bleedin' money, mates
I care about the band
and
making rock music that lives up to the hype
ya ask me?
we should get ambitious, and
talk to George about
making some
landmark
albums
be really ambitious
and
grow
grow musically
and
grow our sound
even if we can't, you know
play
it
live
anymore
the money means diddly-squat
to
me!
I hear ya
yeah
I hear that, too, mate

great point
let's get creative, and
really blow the fans minds right back
the way
they're blowing ours with this
reception
we're getting
agreed
well, hey
guys
I just care about you
you, John
you, Paul
and
you, George
I love you
and
I just wanna make sure
that
we all stay
close, good friends
for
life
you know, I wasn't too popular
back in high school
funny looking, you know
and
I really love you guys
for Pete's sake, I'm
just the drummer
'the funny one', but
I don't want things to get all tossed about between us
that's what I care about

more than anything
truly
really, man
dig?
Ringo, you know
you're
the
most
important member of the band
as
the drummer
I know you can handle it
I got faith in you
and
I wouldn't want anyone else but you
as
our backbone...
friends?
friends!
The Beatles?
The Beatles!!
rock 'n roll!!!

chided for falling into a dilemma

my, my, aren't we a pretty one
there's no other girls like you around here
that's for sure
I like your face
I like your hair
I like your breasts
I like your shorter height and plump build
I admit it'd be nice to touch you here
feel you there
this is not a love poem
this is not a lust poem
this is a war poem
my battle
is with myself
you have very little to do with it
I won't bother you again
but tonight I must say
nobody ever lost for trying,
but nobody ever lost for not trying either
so saunter away
down the neon green sidewalk
and don't forget to
wiggle it
just right…

innocent or guilty

a judge sits in judgment of me
deciding if I can remain free
if I broke the law
if a witness saw
I'm in the hot seat
I'm feeling the heat
24 eyes staring at me
one judge raised above me
they listen to me talk
they try to guess if I'm lying
they got an itchy trigger finger
the victim is crying
the flag is hanging above it all
the president's picture is on the wall
yet I'm the one on trial
these laws don't serve my people
they never were intended to
somebody pays my lawyer
my lawyer is a Jew
the jury's all one color
the opposite of me
somehow I get the feeling this whole circus exists just for them
to feel superiority
my family's wearing suits, and so am I
my family remains quiet while witnesses lie
this whole thing is a foregone conclusion
it's right there in the constitution
3/5s of a man
manifest destiny plan

whites get all the rights
while blacks get hanged by the klan
and live in a garbage can
yet patriotism is enforced
God forbid you don't like sports
and beer and war and guns
I too am America's son
they look at me with slanted eyes
and for some reason they act surprised
that I am even here
I'm the one on trial
but they're they ones in fear
the cops all wear a smirk
for them it's a day off work
the bailiff looks straight ahead
he's seen it a thousand times
the trial of the living dead
accused of minor crimes
it's one big ego trip
everyone feeling the glory
they're looking for any slip
or inconsistency in my story
so they can say, "aha!
we were right all along
he's an evil man
and look he's so strong"
very dangerous indeed
the crime was selling weed
to a suburban teen
he's not on trial at all, it's just me
well I hope you got your rocks off
by sending me away
you want to see me in prison

getting raped by a gay
so you can feel powerful
and like a real sex god
to your fat homely wife
and your mistress with the hot bod
somehow you sleep at night
even though what you do is not right
the whole fucking system is bankrupt
and nobody's trying to change it up
they all just watch the never ending line
even my own kind
are wagging their fingers at me
saying I'm a menace to society
need more Christianity
well, at least we are still free
I'm your Jesus on the cross
society's gain is my loss
throw him in a cell
the white man's heaven is the black man's hell…

the girl of my dreams turned out to be a psycho-hose beast

her name was Maria Covington
I fell in love the instant I glimpsed at her out of the
corner of my eye for a second
she was a million times prettier than any woman I had ever seen,
and
that's no exaggeration
she was so hot I felt like there was
fifty rainbows blasting at my eyes when I looked at her
my heart was palpitating a mile a minute when I rolled up to spit
my game
I trooped on up to her in the bar and
laid down my rap
hey girl
you look good
what say you and me get on the dance floor
and do the horizontal hustle
I wanna check your moves
and see if the candy matches the wrapper
and she responded, without so much as batting an eyelash
aw, damn, dude
buy me a drink first
and stop laying down phony lines
just be yourself, homie
and I replied, almost immediately
damn, girl, why you so stuck up?
can't even talk to a brother unless he's a drug dealer with a
beeper and
a fat gold chain?

and a briefcase full of powdered coke handcuffed to his wrist
or what?
and she kicked her reply without hesitation
man, please
I'm not the one who's stuck up, you're the one who's conceited
you think cause you're really handsome and gorgeous and cute
with
a dope outfit on and all that fly jewelry and a pocket full of cash
and you smell nice
just any girl's gonna talk to you in here?
think again, boy
besides, I got a man
that one hurt, I'll admit it
but I shot back, without dillydallying
yo, girl, peep this, if you please
you look good
I think we could build some kind of interaction level if
you would just get off your high horse and bring it down to earth
once in a while
and you know, just talk
you don't constantly have to put on airs
this is Al, your boy, I love everybody, I'm not gonna bite
and she says, get this, right away she says
boy,
you're cute and all
and that polka dot suit is fly with those pinstriped shirts you're
wearing
but still, you don't know how to mack right
listen,
I need to achieve a comfort level before I can even say hi, much
less accept a drink
from some strange guy who's here picking up women
when I'm not saying whether i'm here to get picked up too, '

not even to myself, cause I'm true
dig?
so, get me a drink
and start all over with, would you like this drink, I noticed you
were licking your lips and scanning the bar as if to say,
I'm thirsty
try that
so, right away, I did that
and you know what?
we really hit it off
her names Angelica Halverstam
and we have been together two months now
it might be love
she could be the one
time will tell
let's just say
I'm having fun
we appear to be having fun
for now
that's all
nothing more
we'll see what happens
later
in the future
in the next few months
by spring
and maybe summer
too
I love the warmth
ahh, flowers
as far as the eye can see…

decline and fall

when did we lose our way?
I see the vultures diving
picking at the bones
no gristle left
the wind is dying now
it's too hot
snakes slither by
they hear nothing
no ears
its dustbowl time again
the crops shrivel from thirst
graves grow weeds
tractors rust
how can you live like that?
then
more friction amongst
the people
this death is slow
I hear a siren
no, it's just a
skinny prairie dog
trying to breathe
the masses have been tricked
they voted wrong
too many times
because we couldn't stand
together
we fall as one
our shadows
survive...

I see no reason to sleep

why have I spoken?
when night cascades around me
the wings of sorrow drenching me in hot sweat
feeling vulnerable
longing to be soothed by you
the queen of my remorse
a creature custom made to reach perfection
like a white cat with a few black spots
purring in the twilight
on the fence between dreaming and awakening
the morning beckons now
with fruitless
tears...

an ode to the forgotten drunk

you sit upon your barstool
in a haze of shattered dreams
with the crust of nightmares old and new
encaked upon your jeans
with one hand on your whisky glass
and one on your cigar
you vaguely muse on where you've been
and also where you are
the jukebox plays a happy song
picked out by someone else
a fool to you perhaps, but cool, to himself
so who's the winner in this tale
of battles to the death?
a drunk with whisky on his mind,
or whisky on his breath?

the source of your power

is it in your words
which tinkle like bells in the still morning
of my essence?
is it in your smile
which teases and warms me
sending a satellite signal of enchantment?
is it in your touch
which sets off a thousand tiny blazes
in my inner mesmerized being?
is it in your laugh
which stutters melancholy, clinking
in the misty dawn?
or is it in your embrace
which holds me still in pure
trembling
motionless
excited
freefall?

an ode to the uptight white

...okay, now you I can't actually celebrate
with an ode, because you traffic hate
so I do not support your side
you horde some guns, and sit and hide
paranoid about the liberals
cause you can't even sympathize a little
even a little, with the suffering of the oppressed
and you yell and howl, and puff your chest
and think you look all sure and mighty
but you are just an average whitey
who thinks that everyone else is wrong
and you're always singing that same old song
the Democrats are gonna take our guns!
the Democrats are gonna crucify nuns!
the Democrats want to open the border
while, hey, the people in Flint still don't have water
and there's systemic racism, which you deny
and call it 'playing the race card' without batting an eye
oblivious to how crazy and stupid you sound
to intelligent people the world around
all you do is criticize
and trample on the little guys
and self-justifying your boorish ways
by then castigating the gays
and basically you have mad anger issues
cause you're so wound up, your ass couldn't even fit a tissue
it's so damn tight with straight-laced ego
and a superiority complex that's extremely fragile
now, all of this just says to me

that people like you just aren't cut out to be free
you'd rather live in a strict, lame realm
where there is no fun, just buy and sell
and minimal free-flowing party folks
and everyone drinks, but no one smokes
until they're numb, and then pass out
and once in a while they chew someone's ass out
as their token ne'er-do-well
to feel supreme, and avoid Hell
which is quite silly a way to live
cause you have no love of others to give
and life to you is one big war
because you just can't bring yourself to hire a whore
and get your rocks off one good time
and for once in your life feel just fine
and not boiling over with self-righteous rage
because your wack ass finally got laid
some of you even need to hire a guy
now I know you'll never give that a try!
and begin to heal your psycho-sexual disorders
and stop being a punk in front of your daughters
cause this just makes them lose faith in men
and the sex worker cycle starts all over again
because they have no strong male role model
just an asshole, clutching a bottle
and sitting there all steamed up and shit
and looking weak cause he does nothing about it
and the whole house feels grim, and full of hate
all the time, from morning 'til late
there never even is one lighthearted moment
and for girls, that's a really sad environment
then this spawns young bullies at their schools
who harass and beat the different, small, and cool

emulating and expressing what you wish you could
and life's pretty bad, when it could easily be pretty good
so, as for your opinions, stick 'em where the sun don't shine
cause your son's smarter than you, and he's only nine
bottom line, you sit on your behind and whine
and the overall effect is you're wasting everybody's time
obsessing about crime
to make a dime
by pleasing your boss, Mr. Ross
then, go home and hit the sauce
and thinking you look like Mr. Big
I would've hated to have to have been your kid
cause here in Chicago, there is no bullies in our schools
and our parent's raised us without too many rules
so, you know what? we know we're right
and you all are just going out like Mr. White...

an ode to the down brown

...hey, there, dude, can I have some food?
I'm feelin' kinda hungry
and can I get a cigarette, too
or would that be too lucky?
of me to get a little help, from you, a passerby?
you see, I'm broke, with no help from my folks
even when I ask her why
I guess my people are just crazy
not too lazy to mail a check
and as for beggin', that's not where I'm headin'
I'm not gonna break my neck
now you seem like the friendly type
and nice, normal, and sane
you can't imagine, how these white dragons
to deal with are such a pain
so, yeah, I guess, that it's my fate
to wait in line for a job
cause I can't fail, by going to jail
because I steal and rob
so, tell me, what's the good life like?
is it all it's cracked up to be?
cause all this dealing, just needs healing
in my white society
I heard that y'all think they are sweet
well, that's completely wrong
most can't even talk at all
their mind must just sing songs
now when it comes to black men like you
a cat like me is really grateful

that there's someone that's not dumb, uptight, and hateful
so, yo, dig this, I got a blunt
would you like to share it?
sure, man, pass it, blunts are classic
and don't forget, you'll probably inherit!

an ode to the lovely Latina

...órale vato, what's happening, wey?
looks like another beautiful day!
here in Chicago, where we dwell
I heard Mexico's a living hell!
but Puerto Rico seems really nice
oh, yeah, give me three steak tacos, with beans and rice
and Coke is fine, I don't drink horchata
to me, it ain't nothin' but cinnamon rice water
so, mira, let's get down to the nitty-gritty
I like your sister, damn, she's pretty!
so can I ask her for a date?
or am I dollar short, and a day late?
does she have an hombre, or a novio?
just tell me straight, man, keep it real!
cause I have to say, I love Latinas!
and I wanna see if I can be a
boyfriend to one, your sister'll do
and me? I'm Middle Eastern, a rich, smart Jew
so I will treat her just like a queen!
so, where's my tacos, rice, and beans?
I'm feelin' hambre, this is true
now tell me what the fuck am I supposed to do?

all people do is give me dirty looks

I'm just homeless, man
I got a right to be poor as dirt
when wages have been stagnant for thirty years
and my whole world is ruled by you know who
nobody cares about nothin no more but bitching
and whining at others for their problems
guess they're right though
everybody's problems are caused by others
their parents and their kids
getting revenge on each other
back and forth
in a big circle jerk
cause they all are a bunch of spoiled sissies
cause they never had anything important happen
that, you know, was relevant to anything that mattered
to the world at large
solving homelessness will take more than just charity
and a serious plan
it will take people who are willing to get down in the mud
people who are willing to get dirty
not only messy
but dirty
dirty hands and dirty feet and dirty clothes even
nobody is willing and able and ready to get that dirty
for a bum
it's not poetic enough
it's not poignant enough
to give their lives meaning
and purpose

and an identity worth having
that's why we have germaphobes
and neat freaks
and bathroom scrubbers
and anal retentives
and obsessive compulsives
and on the other end
hoarders
and faceless people who don't show their face or have egg on
their face
boy is my face red, they used to say
now they say
sorry, no cash
sorry, last one
sorry, but good luck
luck is the major factor in life
to be born in the
right place
at
the
right time
in the right area of that place
in the right family
with the right amount of money, more or less more or less
and with the right community around you
and with the right culture to be exposed to
and with the right way of being parented legal
and with the right friends available to guide and protect you from
all the above
then you can begin to hope
to be the right type of person you'd like to be if you want to be
right
rather than righteous or holy

which is your right
and much more important as a place to start
luck is what you should try to give your kids
luck is what you should gravitate towards and migrate towards
try your luck in a new town
run away from a bad luck situation
lucky is how we should feel when we wake up in the morning
not how we should feel when we go to bed at night like me
a bum
at night we should feel nothing but wearily sleepy and silly
grinning and yawning and stretching and
sated
with
the
day's
events…

an ode to the English language

a plethora of gorgeous faces
a golden visage, lips of graces
I love those freckles
your face is speckled
strawberry blonde, crush my spirit
words and music, beats and lyrics
follow and kill, crimson blood spill
the winter's chill, the old and ill
I need these words, I love these phrases
I can't live in the history pages
nature vs. nurture, back to the future
say my name, say my name rampant murder
European colonization
amazing victories, building nations
what's the point and who fucking cares?
houses with one floor, houses with stairs...

I caught feelings for this girl who stomped on my heart

the thing about Amanda Valentine was
she was so damn pretty
damn!
she looked like a rose and a sunset and a Renaissance painting
times a million
put it this way-
she glowed
iridescent in her glory
a mesmerizing landscape of white and yellow tulips
stretching off into the magenta distance
would be the most apt metaphor
for her extreme good looks
so, I kicked it to her
hardcore
within three seconds of catching a glimpse of her
on the 22 Clark
she was fiddling with her phone
and sipping from a bottle of mountain spring water
I forget which brand
her favorite, no doubt, but
yeah
I stepped to her immediately
not daring to let this one slip away
like a thief in the night
never to return, no
I spit in her face
damn!
you fine!

I'm sorry, lady
but
damn!
you are so pretty!
wow wow wow wow wow golly!
am I hallucinating off strong LSD and seeing
things that don't exist?
I don't remember slipping a tab of strong acid with my morning
cafe au lait…?
from Dunkin Donuts by the train stop
which I have just transferred from, girl!
I mean, holy moly!
you are a vision
in grey and black winter pedestrian commuter coats and scarves!
can you tell I am not kidding around?
you make Marilyn Monroe look like a puddle of puke!
I'm sorry, lady
I just had to let you know that
in all earnest seriousness of regard with my eyeballs
I have 20/20 vision
never needed spectacles
or contact lenses
whether over night or thirty-day varieties
I assure you without lying, that
my eyes work perfectly
both of them
I have two
like most human beings
of the fully functioning variety
two eyes
one heart
one soul
and

right now?
right here?
on the Clark street bus?
my soul is singing!!!
it's 7:20 am
shitty and grey out
with winter
and
you
are a
ray of
golden sunshine smashing
into my eye sockets!
whew!
….beautiful!
please
I got to know your name
I got to meet you with introductions of saying hi good morning
ma'am
how are you doing today, miss pretty face?
and
why is an international super model
riding the CTA
fiddling with her phone
like a common prole?
on her way to the office?
it doesn't make sense, I tell ya, it just don't!
where's the paparazzi?
and the adoring fans
screaming
and shrieking
I love you I'm your biggest fan
and other such outburst of fan club membership at you?

where?
I'm befuddled
you look like a rose among common milkweed plants!
I've got to know your name
I'm Alex
Alex Diamond, the first, of the Chicago Diamonds
you may have heard of us
my dad was a pretty heavy politician
back in the 60s
forget it
listen
I'm Alex, and who might you be, if I may
cause you are stunning
forgive me the impropriety
of interrupting your phone fiddling
and water bottle sipping relaxation
commute to the office
downtown
in a high rise law firm office environment
or even better, young lady?
keeping in mind, I'm Alex
call me Al
if you so choose
and she spoke
hi Alex
my name is
Amanda Valentine
of the Valentines of Wichita originally
but I moved here
to pursue
my dream of a
career in
you guessed it—

litigation!
I am a lawyer!
I do work at a prestigious law firm downtown!
trying cases
and representing
high dollar clients and accounts
in
money court
strictly civil representation
cause criminals are broke!
I wanna be rich, baby
ha ha
nice to meet you
Al
early enough for ya?
how's your coffee cup?
fine fine I replied
warm and brown, sugary
so, tell me, Amanda
where did you attend law school?
and get your lawyering certification approved
by bar passing test achievement?
and she said, dig this, she said
oh
Oxford
the one in England of worldwide note and reputation
since 1548
I was like
wow!
you're a Rhodes Scholar?
damn, lady
beauty beyond compare
and a big juicy brain?

you are a very high-quality individual indeed, if I may say so
myself
I'm a poet
I write
myself
spill my soul
onto the pixelated screen of modern computer pages
for my bread
I eat off my poetry
I made it
I'm a success
at my dream
since the tender age of 12
so, I'm happy
mostly
damn, Oxford, huh?
you must be a super brainiac maniac!
and a litigator
of the highest order!
talkin' big dollar clients
and
at the
young, young, young age
of
oh, I'd say, with my eagle eye
26?
if I may be so presumptuous
to hazard a guess
and she says
yes, Alex
I am indeed 26
you guessed it on the nose
with your guessing ability on point

just then the bus began to rumble under a tunnel
and it got dark in the bus
I was glad
relieved
I needed a break from staring intently
at her beautiful face
and kind eyes
of the coolest blue-grey pools of water
I sipped my coffee
and took a deep breath
this was it
we reentered daylight
and I did it
I asked
so scared, shy, trepidatious, and nervous
so, Amanda
I got to know
will you go out with me?
on a date?
dinner and a movie?
on the weekend?
my treat?
she paused
which caused my heart to pound poundingly
like a jackhammer in concrete
for a split second
she furrowed her brow in the cutest way for a moment
then whispered
yes
I will!
for you see, I always say yes to any gentleman suitor
who requests my company on a date
of dinner and a movie

to be fair
and
generous
with
my precious time
cause I know it's hard for guys
they get so flustered with attraction all the time
I understand
it's physiological
yeah yeah
sure, man
I'm available the 26th of March
a Friday
but
I insist on going dutch
I am a feminist too you know
as a high-powered career woman, I
feel it's incumbent and necessary
oops! here's my stop
take my card, Amanda
I have a card with my contact information even as a published
poet
of some regard
because I like business cards
plus I need them for sub sandwich winning purposes
Amanda
it was great to meet you
you
are
gorgeous!
she rose from her bus seat of many other lessers
and grabbed her briefcase, and adjusted her winter scarf
about her swanlike graceful neck

Alex
I'll see ya on the 26th of this month
shit
this is my stop
no time for the even exchange of business cards
but I work
at
Leiberman, Gary, Fitz, Monroe and Jefferson
Attorneys at Law
I haven't made partner yet
I'm only 26
bye!
I think
I am
in love
Amanda
will be hearing from me
that's for certain
I love beautiful women!
Chicago is
my
home…

we just clownin' up in here

you swear up and down we're not?
that's your claim?
no doubt about it?
absolutely positive?
sure as shit, you might say?
totally one hundred percent decided
not a tiny iota of a shred of a qualm about this point in
your mind, is that so?
you know, Al and his buddy Chuckie are not clowning?
in other words, you disagree, with the assessment
you've made, through
intense observation, and taking copious notes, that Al is
NOT just fuckin' illin'!?
we got so many honeys comin' through it's like a
landslide!
we're buried in girlies, me and Chuck!
you can't believe it!
but you better believe it!
it's on like Donkey Kong over here at Al's spot, yo
utter mayhem!
anarchy times chaos times a billion it's so live!
you just don't realize how goddam dope our whole
entire radical chic scene is, and
it's bumpin'!
why do you dispute that fact so vehemently?
when it's as apparent as the nose on my face that I'm
fuckin' flippin'!!
I'm gettin' down like Charlie Brown!
and gettin' ill like Wild Bill, y'all!

yee-haw!!
I swear up and down on fifty million stacks of Bibles we
are wildin' out, joe
like a motherfuck, man!
this shit is so crazy, bro!! goddam, man!
yeah, so come by, man!
bring drugs!
brink drinks!
bring food!
bring cigarettes
and bring lube and condoms and your video cameras
too!!!
Al straight gets down, brah
dude, he's bad as hell
he does shit right
yeah, son
hey, wait, wait, don't open your mouth to
disagree! don't do it!
no!
yes!
I cede the floor…

scary man speaks

what is the major difference between life and death?
sleep and awake?
heaven and hell?
night and day?
love and hate?
I don't know
but, I think that it has something to do with darkness and
light
light representing life
awareness
a conscious
see, in life we have to take chances
and there is no escape from the clutches of luck
or the cliffs of happenstance
so leap
leap in to the great hereafter
oblivion in the mists of eternity
this is not a dream
this is life
unbound...

an ode to fallen poets

your grizzled life and fizzled wife
have left you on your own
without a doubt, without a clue
and even without a phone
in some forgotten New York dump
you lay there on your bed
in a semi-catatonic state
with flies around your head
with broken records, broken dreams
and stains upon your love sheets
a poem's just a poem, man
it doesn't have to have a beat
now if you had the chance to do it all over again
perhaps you wouldn't steal five bucks
from your one true friend
and modern music has a way
of slipping through our grasp
but it more than slipped away from you
it kicked you in the ass!
trooping through the littered streets
you swear you're on the prowl
but no one cares about
a master of the vowel who wears a scowl
so pin your hopes on one thing
your city if that seems best
but your city can do more than just get hyped
it can put a bullet in your chest..!

the martyrs of cowboy culture

…broken moments in the span of time
I'm met with much resistance
the way I feel
like less than human
it's hard
pumping poems out is not my style
yet it would be nice to
write more often, but
eh, it just ain't like that
knowing how most people approach it
like taking a piss, they do five a day, not me
trying wouldn't help
lying wouldn't help
even crying wouldn't help
wanna make a dent, but
when it came time to make my book, I
found I only had 37
well, no matter
all I know is what I know, no more no less, still
the words aren't there
they're lost
maybe they slipped out of my pocket on the bus, on the train
what I need
is
love
love
and
experiences
that are meaningful, that arouse my passion
it's a big world out there

more than 200 countries, all different
maybe I should go see one
two
three
four
what good is a man of letters if he only knows his own backyard,
I ask
I ask that, man
really
I need to branch out, see new things, new faces and new places
I'm in a rut here
I need to travel!
France
England
Spain
Italy
China and Japan
I'd like to go to Israel, and Egypt, too
that's about it
then?
then?
maybe I'll know something about life and love and letters,
literature…
cause America hasn't shown me much, to tell the truth, not much
at all…
it's some honky-tonk shit…
everybody wants to be a cowboy, a crusader, left and right wings
both…
they care about politics, passionately
they march for it, they riot for it, they kill for it
don't they know what's up?
I mean, it's obvious to me
clear as day
the biggest problem we have can't be solved

never will be, either
it's intractable
it's impossible
when your country is full of guns, your country is full of murders
that's all
and the 2nd Amendment will always be kept
there's nothing we can do about it
so many murders, it's an outrage, it's a tragedy, it's a holocaust
they might have killed my wife, my future friend, my hero, or my
savior!!
it's an outrage
and nothing
nothing can stop the killing
nothing
no way, no how
and I'm not desensitized, I'm not numb to it, it still bothers me!
when you know how amazing people can be?
a wasted life is a fucking outrage!
it's a fucking disaster!
haven't you heard them sing, haven't you heard their songs?
humans?
some of their songs are so great!
don't take a life that could've made an incredible song, incredible
music, you asshole!
I need music!
I love music
I love it!
you monsters!
you have no idea
you have no idea what you waste when you kill someone
they could've done anything that's ever been done and more, and
you
you, you spoiled brat
you little maggot

you took them from the earth, from humanity, from me, and from
everyone!
you bastard!
I don't care if you're a killer cop or a killer killer
you suck!
fuck you, man!
fuck you!
and the horse you rode in on, bastard!
scum!
so
yeah
yeah, man
men of murder
yeah
no
so
so, as it stands, this is not a land of love
it's not
a civilized land
a land of peace
and a land of beauty
and a land of love
love, like I need it to be
like we all need, need and wish it to be
love
cause
there is no poetry in hate, in murder, in violence
none at all
I said this years ago
I wrote the president
and
my senator
I really did
when I first started writing poems

20 years ago
I said, please, stop the violence!
end the carnage!
I want to be a poet, and
I need beauty
to
write about!
ugliness doesn't work!
they never wrote back
I wonder why
I'll tell you why
cause they know
they know there's no solution
there's nothing we can do
cause guns are here to stay
that's all
that's all we can count on
somebody will be killed tonight
and tomorrow
and Thursday, too
I'm sorry
I failed
them
the bodies
the fallen
the martyrs of cowboy culture...
I failed them, man
they're gone forever
we failed them
we all failed them
we failed them all
America
us...

Magna Carta

see
the world
Earth
dropped the ball
in
1215
when Europeans wrote
the Magna Carta
and
the king signed it
they should've immediately predicted
everything
pushed the king out
and
installed a leader from the population
freed the people as much as feasible
and invested in their students with a spark for science
(including tech and engineering and psychology)
and math
everybody else should have been
freed from censorship
or
sheltering
and
allowed full learning
and
expression
and
opportunity to manifest themselves

of their talents
without
exploitation
or
punishment
we then needed to find a way
to
peacefully plunder nature
for chemicals
every chemical imaginable
worldwide ocean deep
all starting in
1215
we needed to encourage and support
artists
and
philosophers
and
teachers
and
famous leaders
to use their platform and voices
to break down
societal
and
social
and
familial
and
community
and
personal
pressures

from
restrictive traditions
and
philosophies
pseudoscience
and
wrong-headed
or
damaging
ideas and philosophies
and
unnecessary honor codes
and
fixing
egotism
greed
homophobia
sexism
misogyny
racism
xenophobia
anti-semitism
Islamophobia
colonial ideals and plans
empire
genocidal impulses
strictness and discipline
anal retentiveness
self-esteem bipolarity
hate
jealousy
fear
rigidity and close-mindedness

machismo
all our sexual psychoses
violent impulses
male rage and bloodlust
apathy
nihilism
self-sabotage
shyness
bullying
sociopathic tendencies
oedipal complexes
conformist impulses
mob mentality
panic impulse
denial and avoidance and overcompensation
which are also self-esteem issues
lazy thinking
fear of failure
unhappy success
environmental neglect
backwardness and barbarism
lack of civility and friendliness
tamed hierarchy
and
then
built
universities of
science and technology
all over the world
and
dedicated ourselves
to
never wasting

any human's
life or mind
or
time
or
restricting
their
total
autonomy
at
all...

here for the hot hunt

no remorse
no delay
no exceptions
I have always felt like
this is going to get good
now things are finally looking up
I brokered a major deal
I landed a big account
anyway if you don't think I got what it takes
I do I do I really do!
you see, these minor obstacles
are all par for the course
in between things build up, then crest
foam away into nothingness
cold clean water is the medicine
drink it often
drink some now
I'll be waiting for you
in my
boots and belt
calm and content
another puff of smoke
then... victory!

an ode to Jew boy weakness

...you guys are really fucking dumb
to assume my heart was always numb
and that is your excuse to hold my nuts
and that is your excuse to fuck your sluts
and that is why you just don't get it
cause you just live for extra credit
and feeling like a big old hero
for passing a school test and not getting a zero
like maybe you should get a life
and stop worrying about your future wife
and whether she proves you're not gay
and brushing your teeth for tooth decay
instead of for the washing feeling
and prayer's for talking, not for healing
because it looks a little funny and small
to be throwing eggs upon or against the wall
like a kid who's trying to get laid
when he's only in the first or second grade
come on now, boy, don't be such a clownish fool
when all you ever knew you learned in school
life is what it takes to make a dent
and life contains much more than paying rent
it's full of hope and joy and love and sorrow
when all you ever dreamed ain't there by tomorrow
and nobody seems to know the master plan
and there's so many drunken uncles in your clan
and all you really want is a room of your own
with a nice TV, a bed, and a cellular phone
to call so many friends you can talk all night

and somebody just takes a chance and says you're bright
and if nobody does it's not that big a deal
but it just goes to show you should never kneel
cause when you pray, you are reflecting the truth
which is that God resides among the youth
in fact, the boys, the boys are where he stays
so don't ever kneel down when you start to pray
cause everyone around the world can see it
and it really makes them mad when they have to be it
the one who dies to prove Jew boys ain't playin'
yes, God is real and he never needs obeying
except of course if you don't know the way
and ask Him for His guidance on Christmas Day
cause that's the time when everyone's having fun
so that's the worst time to shoot your gun
cause now they all know that you are pissed
at missing all the toys that were on your list
which means that you were out celebrating both
and now nobody knows if you need some clothes
because as God has said, we all get dressed
so if your gear ain't comfy, give it a rest
and stop trying to get a Jew boy to quiet down
and just admit to yourself that you feel like a clown
who can't really ever control his fate
cause cops and soldiers suck, but it ain't too late
for you to hopefully one day get a real job
and stop disappointing the girls by dressing like a slob
who doesn't even know it's not New Year's Day
and lives his whole life worrying about who is gay
cause that's the worst thing a man can do
just waste his time never pondering nothing new
but always obsessing about if somebody's gay
until he misses out on the New Year's Day

when he could've got a kiss and sealed the deal
and learned to never pray when you have to kneel
and that's as far as God needs you to take it
but maybe once or twice pray when you are naked
and even pray when you feel like a jerk
like in your monkey suit on the way to work
remember to pray then too, if you can recall it
so that you can give thanks for the cash in your wallet
which is there to buy you food and shelter and toys
and musical records and guitars to jam with your boys
that means the time you spend may not be worth it
but still in all you should feel that it is perfect
to make a joyful noise unto the Earth
and celebrate your life for what it's worth!

the upside of all this mess is redemption

I didn't shoot the guy!
I was running, running fast
and
there was a crack, a boom, a blast
I didn't know which way to turn, at first
so, I ducked into an alley, to catch my breath
I heard dogs barking nearby
there was puddles everywhere, and I was
afraid I might slip, my feet were wet
my socks were soggy, and
I was winded
I needed a rest
I couldn't breathe
my lungs were burning
and all this noise of sirens was surrounding me
what the hell was going on?
I didn't know
I just wanted to get home, and lock the door
I wanted to hide
I wanted to strip naked
and lay back on the couch, in warmth
and
forget that any of this ever happened
I wanted to drink a coke
then some coffee
I was hungry, too
I wanted chocolate
yes, at a time like this, I did
I thought of delicious food

I thought of dryness and warmth, like I said
but I was lost
not geographically, in my city
no
I was at a loss for how to escape the dogs
and
the sirens
wailing and screeching like hell-hounds
but
there was nothing to be done
they found me
and took me here
I didn't do it
I'm not like that
I'm not violent
it had to be someone else
maybe my ghost
I don't know
I don't know
I really don't know…

the most important thing in life to be is holy

the way to be holy
is by retaining your self-respect
and pride
and dignity
and sense of self-worth
out of awe at God's best creation- man
yourself
there may be even greater rewards
on other paths
but there is guaranteed
greater suffering
and avoiding suffering
is what life is all about
gaining happiness
is only possible
when you have eliminated suffering
in your life
and this is never a simple job
unless you are a simpleton
and being one is anathema to worshipping man
which is more important
than worshipping God
because to worship God
takes only faith in your heart
but to worship man
takes love in your soul
the smallest soul
can have the biggest love
and the biggest heart

can have the meanest soul
but
the biggest man is not always the most loving
the biggest man is the most forgiving
and God wants you to be the biggest and most forgiving
man
you can be
so you can love your fellow man even when he is wrong
and hurts you
because all mankind is always in need of more love
no matter how much they may already have
there's never such thing as too much love
there's never such thing as too many souls forgiven and
loved
man is good as much as the land allows and man has
sometimes pushed for more
and that is enough for God
to know that man is Loving
and now we will see
if man is
forgiving
if he has
love
in his soul
as well
as
in
his
societies
enough
to stop
killing
and

stealing
and
raping
and hurting with systems of inequality and subjugation
institutionalized
and reform
rearrange
and
reeducate
and
rehabilitate
and
renovate
and
revive
and someday
reinvigorate
because that is the society
that most pleases God
one that is invigorated
because that's how mass love makes individual men and
women and children
feel
vigorous
which comes from
victorious
constant victory
produces
vigorousness
living life with the
energy
of
zest

is
what
God
the only God there is
wants
from
human beings
to be alive with pleasure
because you are a winner
so you have vigor
as
an
attitude
instead
of
mannish
rebellion
and
grief
love is great
and vigorously
is
how
you
should
love…

just trust lust and you must bust out justice

...well, all is under smooth control
the kid is bringing back the soul
and rock and roll is on the way
and all will be cool by this May
people from west coast to east
finally will all live in peace
loving daughters and their sons
loving life not loving guns
and if you think I can't make it happen
then you must not have heard real rappin'
like the hypeness of Kool Keith
who stole the show like a jewel thief
or like the songs of KRS
who got the dope stuff off his chest
5 or 6 anthems of cop killing
cause those pigs should have never been willing
to sacrifice one person's life
so I could choose art and not my wife
so if you think love is not required
then you must not know real desire
just buzzing on some ego trip
with gun or wallet on your hip
cause love is what it takes for kids
and rebel art makes prison bids
then all that's left is sex for sale
and society is all for the male
and as for living real dope life
you only dream of meat and knife
and can not think of nothing wild

because you do not have a child
with a hope of doing well
and life becomes a prison cell
a living hell of pain and fear
and cigarette and weed and beer
and all this money which you lack
and all the whites hold back the blacks
and then you see just what occurred
the land became the domain of nerd
and square and geek and religious fraud
and you have no girlfriend and no broad
no other reason that you live
will ever measure up to give
more excitement to behold
you sold your heart for tears of gold...

to do list

get shower and toilet fixed
buy deodorant-wear it
do laundry
call Women and Children First
pay cable bill
look online for jobs
become perfect
quit smoking
exercise
quit eating meat
recycle
get a haircut
shave off your beard
jump off a bridge
manscape
buy some shorts
put a little love in your heart
learn to care
learn to think of others more than yourself
revolt
solve everything
be a man
sacrifice yourself
immolate yourself
paint graffiti
check yourself
commit class suicide
waste more time
get a woman

get women for all the guys you know
be quiet
kill yourself
hang yourself
draw less
stop writing
be scared
live up to your potential
become a DJ
leave the country
leave the planet
change your style
quit biting
talk with an accent
stop drinking cokes
stop supporting large corporations
stop wasting paper
apologize
to the earth
and everyone on it
pray for forgiveness
study history
fight for Palestine
don't say anything
kill some people then yourself
learn to cook
learn to clean
quit being disappointing
be somebody else
get married
start a family
raise kids
free your mind

learn everything
blend in
fit in
don't ruffle feathers
stop ruffling feathers
get your priorities straight
organize your life
brush your teeth
go to the dentist
go to the doctor- get a check up
adopt a baby or child
shave your head
get the air conditioner from Tyler
live more for others
quit being greedy
get a job
waste less time
waste the right time
take a good long look at yourself
thoroughly clean this crib-get rid of bed bugs
buy new mouse traps
throw away bike
recycle Jewel bags
learn to empathize with assholes
record a song on the 8 track
send package to Allen Fiscus
stop enjoying yourself
humble yourself
enter reality
wake up
act your age
don't just sit there
get off Facebook

do what other people want you to do
live for others
die for others
fight for others
stay away from others
be sad
get angry
go back to college
call your mother
visit your mother
visit your sister and nieces and nephews
learn to have discipline
learn cursive
learn Spanish
buy some clippers
get off your ass
grow the fuck up, quick
stop playing
stop playing Mr. Innocent
move away from Chicago
move away from the north side
go out on the town
go to a club
go to a party
go to a concert
go to Michigan
stop talking shit
quit excusing yourself
quit making excuses
learn to communicate
learn to converse
learn to learn
pray to Jesus Christ

pray to God
learn to start worrying
join up with a team
join the mainstream
quit making people jealous
wash your ass
wash your hair
learn to watch movies
clear your mind
start meditating
stop joking
denounce yourself
open your heart
stop guessing
stop judging
stop criticizing
change yourself
save yourself
adjust your attitude
be responsible
be serious
suffer for others
be everybody's Jesus for them
save humanity
hang on a cross
stand up to the Romans
quit being typical/ stereotypical
give it up
learn to think
quit thinking about bullshit
learn to hate people hate/ groups
learn what other people's expectations are of you, and live up to
them

stop swearing
go climb a tree
go to the beach
go to the movies
go on a date
mack to a woman on the street
quit jerking off
watch more viral videos
empty out your ashtray
buy a gun
shoot someone, then yourself
get tough
lift weights
learn a martial art
teach a photography class
teach an art class
teach a rap music class
read the Joey Ramone book
improve your posture
stop trying
denounce European culture
question everything
quit being a scumbag
get a tattoo
for God's sake, hurry up
put your books away
finish writing the Medusa's screenplay
start a revolution
assassinate Scalia
follow the rules
go to law school
go skydiving
quit smoking weed

quit arguing
stop enjoying yourself
quit looking at the big picture
leave everybody alone
quit feeling sorry for yourself
learn to feel sorry for others
eat three meals a day
learn to sing better
stop rapping
stop freestyling
stop making beats
stop writing poems
stop playing
wise up
learn to hear your thoughts
go on a diet
throw out your coke bottle collection
call Shun, apologize
open up a can of worms
quit confusing positive and negative
look in the mirror
take some pride in yourself
have some shame
quit being sexist
buy a car
grow some weed
take over Michigan house
start a fight with Uncle Lou
learn to have a reaction
quit being blase
quit being aloof
quit changing the subject
stop patronizing others

ignore the homeless
be all things to all people
quit fuckin' crying
learn to laugh-you don't laugh
get some new friends
call Peks
Call Qortez about website
start blog
join the mafia
join the army
move to NYC
move to LA
move to SF
move to DC
move to Glenn
stop agreeing
learn to dream
be ruthless
save some money
whack someone
be yourself
be better than yourself
quit using your mind
use your body- harder, not as lazy
learn to dance
wipe that "screwface" off- you ain't hard
learn new tricks, old dog
watch your mouth
ignore assholes, if possible
run and hide
take your meds
get on a regular sleep schedule
wear your watch

quit being confused
focus!
look people in the eye when you talk to them
relax
keep your eye on the important stuff
don't ignore your surroundings
get feelings
get out of denial
try to stop congratulating yourself
humble yourself
stop cutting corners
quit forgetting things
quit trying to sell art for money (waste of time)
learn to feel people and their vibe
resume guitar lessons
give or throw guitar away
act like you know what you're doing
act your age- 41 years old
don't be so lost, be found
stop having fun while others are suffering
get on a schedule, not a rut
get peddler's license
try cutting your wrists again
learn to feel people out
trim your beard
stop writing to do lists
stop gripping African America
stop stealing Latina women
have some honor
stop being cynical and proud
stop lying
take a look at yourself
simplify yourself

focus
quit trying to change others, change yourself
be brave
accept the world on it's own terms
expand your horizons
stop giving away secrets
buy socks and underwear
be more aware of your immediate surroundings
stop procrastinating!!!
put stamps on pictures, put in stores
stop doing pointless shit
stop being pretentious about your art
quit being a poser
listen to your conscience
fix your life as much as possible
appraise your life/situation accurately
learn to sit for movies
learn to do street photography (people)
go to Doug's opening
get your mind right
call Deal
stop thinking bullshit
face your fears
get hard
stop being soft
try to learn to think realistically about yourself, the world, your
future
stop fucking with people
love people...

a mere trifle

Al Capone not a def poet, is what you're saying?
worthless garbage suitable for the land fill
utter nonsense, putrid scribble scrabble
total yammering, in other words
that's what you're postulating?
just toss it right in the trash
in a fraction of a second
without even a whisper of regret
bottom line?
okay
fine
you're much better, then
is your claim
out write Al in a New York minute, by and large
that's your fiercest opinion and you believe that
to the very core of your being
right into your very living breathing soul
Al, garbage, you, great
that's the reality
is your pedigree and family crest?
okay
so
Al needs to burn all his pens and poems
in a giant flaming bonfire that can be seen from space
is the best plan
according to your assessment
and all the knowledge you hold so dear
give it up, DJ Al Capone!
your poems suck!

and you don't know shit from shinola
about writing
this your sure of
is what you feel, right?
as sure as you're sitting there, you know
Al can't write!
it's so obvious, it's
like a thousand suns blasting orange light
right into the very iris of your retina from two feet away it's so
plain to see
that's what you are positing here
right now
loud and clear as a bell without a fraction of a doubt
and utterly not a millisecond's hesitation, right? right?
great, okay
fine
I see
well
good then
Al should just forget he even speaks English
and learn Esperanto, or sign language, bottom line
and totally give up the ghost fast
in a quick hurry speedy like lightning is what you need me to
know
I suppose?
that's your testimony, in this supreme court of law and your oath
to the western world at large and in specific
from the Atlantic to the Pacific
as far as the poetry of DJ Al Capone, right?
sure of this like a prophecy that happened yesterday, right?
you just know— Al Capone sucks at poetry, right?
can't even form a sentence by and large, right?
basically, a mute, a dummy, a stiff, a test tube baby

that's what you got in your diary and column of your
poetry critiquing, eh?
you know that like the back of your hand, right?
worst poet in world history, this Al Capone character
truth be told?
worse than ten thousand nails screeching down a chalkboard
to hear even one line of Al's verse, right?
can't stand the sound or sight on the page
of his mad scribblings for two seconds, that's what
you want the world to know, screaming from the
rooftops of the tallest skyscrapers in Kuala Lampur, basically
right?
the Petronas Tower, knock it down and build a warning light sign
stay away from DJ Al Capone's books of poetry, world!
you're dedicated to that project so hardcore
you can literally taste it in your mouth, right?
okay
okay
fine
well, fuck you!
I'm good, man!
so incredibly amazing that it's almost unfathomable to the naked
eye
can't even be seen like ultraviolet light, god damn it
is the bare reality
as far as what I think about my shit
truth be told
bet
no doubt
no question
no denial
chisel it on my gravestone
is how I assess myself

damn it
now
I thank you for your time
and
eyeballs
English speaking world
peace!
see ya later...

my gun is my only friend

as I lay reminiscing
about a life that was doomed from the start
I think about the people I knew
and the times that we all shared
and I ponder
what does it all mean?
does anything matter at all?
was I so bad?
was I at all good?
when the shit went down, I handled business
when the money came in, I partied hard
when the law cracked down, I maintained my dignity
all I ever wanted was some love
and a little baby to call my own
things spiraled out of control
anarchy replaced peace
there were explosions and mayhem
lives were snuffed out in an instant
and I always held my ground
now, I feel
now, I wish
now, I live
now, I live
now, I live in my
heart…

a riot grrrrrl! stole my heart

I met Babs O'Hannigan at a protest
she was holding a sign that had a picture of Chef-Boy-Ar-Dee
Spaghettios on it
and
underneath was written
this is not an abortion!
I was smitten
I put down my bullhorn and headed in her direction
ready to get the 411
on
whether or not she was a lesbian
or
maybe a celibate man-hating feminist who was cursed to be
heterosexual
I couldn't tell by looking at her
she didn't have the hardened steely square resting face of a
diesel dyke
but
she also didn't look overtly feminine
or
too
enamored with men, in general, on our planet here
in this era
and being aware of all history and epochs previous
as if to say
she looked woke
so, I was trepidatious as I approached
much like a big game hunter on safari in Africa
sidling up to a majestic lioness

I made my move
hi
I like your sign
it makes me hungry
and pissed
do you deign to consort with the male half of the species?
or are you a die hard female supremacist
who feels reticent to scrape men off the bottom of her shoe?
after all this horror and mishigos
we've perpetrated
on man child
through the years?
tell me, cause
I think you're adorable
looks wise
and refreshingly intimidating
politically
brain-wise?
heart-wise?
different folks lead with different vital organs
but I'd say you're more
of a feeler
than a thinker
here at this activism protest demonstration we're throwing
against oppression
and for
rights
girl
what's your name?
I'm Al
and she said
ahem
um

Al
but, yes
I do fraternize with the violent gender
males
like you
I don't draw the sex line
I am committed to fair and gentle treatment
for all mankind
men
women
children
toddlers
infants
and grannies all the same
so
hi
I'm Babs
Babs O'Hannigan
nice to make your acquaintance
Al
Al
Al what?
what's your surname, Mr.?
and I said
ah, Diamond
it's
a family name
not important
so, Babs
how did you hear about this
rights
protest demonstration we
are throwing here today?

underground resistance intel?
or, Facebook?
I was informed about this march
by my step-sister
Lucretia
myself
she's a radical
she goes to radical protest demonstration marches
all the time
she feels compelled
to do her part
call it a duty
she has kids
daughters
Belle and Priscilla P
she does anything she can to fix up the world right quick so they
will
have good lives
with no
oppression
or
subjugation
or
harassment
or
discrimination
of any kind
her daughters are Puerto Rican
young ladies
of the Latina race
so, she
feels extra protective of them
against

prejudice treatment
or
truncated outcomes
being that they're Puerto Rican and all
plus, obviously, female women of the feminine gender identity
and physiology
girls
as one would say colloquially
tweens
kiddos, man
she
told me about it
that's her over there
holding that protest slogan sign
and chanting a chant of
liberation
she's waving at us right now
her, right there
with the sign
that's her
hi Lucretia!
lookin' good!
yeah
so
how?
and Babs said back to me
sources
put me up on the scoop
and further research
on my part
independently on
the computer internet superhighway
filled in all the missing pieces

till I knew
where
and
when
to show up
with my pasta abortion sign
for rights
I march in solidarity
with my sisters
on a regular consistent basis
as if to say, I care
about my world
our planet
and all her inhabitants
even dung beetles
but especially
women
like
me
and
my friends, and family
and fellow citizens of the US country
all over the midwest
and extending
out to
points continental
throughout the US vicinity
especially
I'm pretty hardcore
I eat meat
but only kosher
even though I'm Presbyterian by birth
the humane breeding and humane slaughter methods,

endorsed by Rabbi Shmuly Rosenberg
are
enough
for
me
bitches gotta eat! ha ha
so, yeah
but
I don't wear fur coats anymore
or mink stoles
or chinchilla wraps tucked up under
my neck
in the cold cold winter's chill, anymore
and the wind
haven't in years
and
I give my cats
real tuna
and
half and half cream to
drink
with their cute little pink sandpaper tongues
I love my kitties!
do you have any pets?
but I'm a riot grrrrrl!
so
I must put on a tough front
especially at these political march protest demonstration meetings
of activism we
keep having
in case any
nazis
wanna

go crazy
and attack me
at
this
event
for being a lefty
who fights back
against
sexism
and
misogyny
with the blood of a fierce amazon warrior princess
goddamnit!
yeah
got to watch out for nazis
they like to hide
and then spring out
at the moment of victory
and try to
kill or maim you
if you are too
hardcore
like me
Babs O'Hannigan
riot grrrrrl!!
to this
I replied
damn!
you are tough
and
strong
and
proud

and
wise
and
fierce
Babs, the amazing amazon rioting grrrrrrrl!!
I should like to take you out on a date
for food and entertainment style
culture
at your earliest convenience
you won my respect
with your spaghetti fetus picture
and you won my attraction
with your gorgeous face and alluring physique and cutting edge
fashion sense
and
shaved purple hair
which not only looks sexy
it shows
you are interesting
an artist?
indubitably
probably makes her own clothes
was my initial reaction to
your punk rock cool kid funky fresh
outfit
and I said
that girl's cool
I'm gonna talk to her
that was two minutes ago
Babs
and now, my plan has come to fruition
we are at the precipice of
finding out if you will bless me

with
the pleasure
of
your company
on a date
to an eating establishment
here
in the city of Chicago
Illinois
and
an entertainment venue
afterwards
so
we may indulge
in
culture
which will give us something to chew on and digest and enjoy
and masticate on
besides
the cuisine fare
which we consume with gusto
as
a
precursor
to
that
plus
we are not cavemen troglodyte neanderthals
not by long shot
we read
we peruse
cause we are cosmopolitan?
eh

hardly
cause we are human
we have brains
and
hearts
far more advanced
than the simple
eat play fuck
of
the average dolphin
in the waters off the coast of the Eastern Seaboard
near Cape Hatteras, North Carolina
humans
so
we enjoy exposing ourselves to culture
of our times
and
society
such as it is
to enlighten
entertain
educate
edify
elucidate
and
feed our souls!
this ain't nascar country here
in
Chicago
left turns and crashes, with survival guaranteed by seat belts and
safety roll bars cages, no
we need meat!
for our minds

then
we
regurgitate it
with our own spin
affected by
our talent
experience
taste
and
unique perspective
boom!
seems like a life
so, I'm afraid the conservatives will never
convince us
or sway us
one iota
with their lazy, disrespectful, conniving, alarmist, reactionary,
punitive, repressed, uptight
jibber-jabber
ha
no
yes
we will remain
hardcore lefty radical artists and revolutionaries
till we win!
and
peace
justice
and
equality
cover the land
from
sea

to shining
sea!
liberty or death!
that's the riot grrrrrl! credo
that I, Babs, ascribe to whole-heartedly
and to my ultimate core
my heart and soul
any questions?
um
Al?
nope
I agree
democratic socialism must win the day!
let's have that date this upcoming Friday night
and eat hearty kosher meats
of the humane variety
and be dazzled by
excellent
cultural arts
performances
and then
snuggle
as we discuss
and
break down
our feelings and
reactions
to
the play, Babs, yes?
which we just saw?
at a small radical theater oblique
as per our orientation to events in the current dialectical milieu?
hmm she said
hmm

dinner
a play
and the company and conversation of one Al?
hmm
hmm
hmm
well
okay
I'll take a chance
you seem genuine
and
sincere
that you really want to show me a good time and enjoy my
presence
without undue pressure for a kiss
or to hold hands
I'll do it
Friday is fine
here's my number
(773) 674-8369
call me
at your leisure
and we can make the final and necessary arrangements
for our date
pleased to meet ya, Al!
same here, Babs! I look forward to this weekend with much
anticipation and flop sweats, Babs
thanks for agreeing
and
I'll call ya later
bye!
to which she replied
1 2 3 4!

we don't want your oil war!
hey ho hey ho
oil wars have got to go!
with her bloody fetus pasta sauce sign
raised high and mighty
then she kissed me on the cheek a peck
and said
bye cutie!
I'm Babs
a riot grrrrrrrl!
I go on dates with guys
cute ones are better
you're cute
see ya!
I was head over heels
at this point
far beyond smitten
and the kiss on the cheek
had my stomach doing cartwheels
but I held on
and maintained
Friday hurry up and get here!
I wanna
see
that girl
Babs O'Hannigan
of the shaved purple hair
I can't wait!
I wonder if
Michael Jordan's Steakhouse
is
kosher....?

low below the earth, a rumble

these days are not the last of the end times
no, this is a commencement party!
things like this never last forever
peace and prosperity and good times will be back
things will be great finally
you know it
we were all born at just the right time
we are all so so lucky to be here right now
computers
capitalism
cigarettes
music for free
porn for free
warm climate
sunshine through my windows
scattering the grey grey blues like a whirlwind
and yes, I did my bit
yes, I took some risks
maybe showed some balls
to make it happen
I participated
I joined the crowd for once
and felt apart of my country in my truncated fashion
it's my years
my era
and my life
this is it!

so let's have love for all humanity!

I'm writing this one right now!
I am not waiting one second!
and
if you think this poem doesn't matter?
then you are pretty stupid!
then you are a pretty stupid
and
violent
right-winger!
not only a bad seed
cursed to be
flesh of my flesh
bone of my bone
and
blood of my blood
which I have to deal with the guilt of creating
but
also
you are my progeny!
and I have to make sure you wind up
in showing the truth
of your
mule-headed stubbornness
because
well
I hate to say this, but...
male
fake
certainty
is the culprit!

is the danger
all the danger!
a huge danger for all mankind!
love!
not hate, but love!
love!
love is the answer!
I know this is the deal!
I know what's up!
so
what's up, you guys out there?
hey!
I got a question for ya…
why?
why?
why?
why are you killing everyone in sight all the damn time, man?!
I know why!
yeah, I know why!
guys
it's cause you suck!
I'm sorry, but
yeah
that's why, sorry to say!
but
yes
I mean, okay, like
what is so hard to understand about that, guys?
men?
love!
love!
love!
love is the answer
and

love is never stubborn
or
donkey-like
or
mule-mugged
lovers!
love
is
free
and
loose!
yeah you guys!
that's the truth, man!
yep
so…
now
I have shown you my heart
my steady beating
red-blooded
heart of love
so
now
tell me, please
go ahead
and
tell me
tell me
what
is
love
to
you?
well..?